finding words

Also by Merle Feld

Poetry and Prose
A Spiritual Life

Plays
Across the Jordan

Merle Feld

finding words

URJ PRESS • New York, New York

Published by:

URJ Press
633 Third Avenue
New York, NY 10017-6778

(212) 650-4120
press@urj.org

Library of Congress Cataloging-in-Publication Data

Feld, Merle, 1947-
  Finding words / Merle Feld. -- 1st ed.
      p. cm.
  ISBN 978-0-8074-1162-9
  I. Title.
  PJ5055.21.E425F56 2010
  892.4'17--dc22

                                      2010036860

Book design by Judith Stagnitto Abbate / Abbate Design

This book is printed on acid-free paper.
Copyright © 2011 by Merle Feld
Manufactured in the United States of America
10 9 8 7 6 5 4 3 2 1

Blessed be the One who spoke

and the world came into being.

B'reishit

Each year we sit expectantly,
waiting to hear how it all began.
We strain and stretch ourselves,
not to imagine darkness, chaos—
darkness and chaos are states
with which we are well acquainted.
No, we begin

by trying to conjure first light,
form and order and sense emerging
from *tohu va-vohu*. And how can it be
that on Day One there was light,
night and day, but sun and moon
not till Day Four? OK, we think,
put aside that question for the moment

as we struggle to see how it was, for light
has limitless possibilities to consider—
shimmering white heat of the Negev,
June sunset over the Pacific, the way it sparkles
on early morning maple leaves
in Maine woods when everything
seems new and promising.

And yes, before sun and moon, the Yangtze,
Ganges, Nile, Mississippi, Danube, North Sea,
Finger Lakes, Victoria Falls, Ein Gedi.
And fig trees, fuchsia, redwood, rhubarb, eucalyptus,

birch, blueberries, mango and mustard seed,
dogwood, dill, the mighty oak, oregano, arugula,
climbing roses, cinnamon and cyclamen.

A fifth day brings us dolphin and wren, duck
and swan, seagull and whale, crocodile, crab,
bat, octopus, butterfly, sockeye salmon and shark,
trout, snapping turtle, blue jay, hawk and dove,
ladybug, lobster, falling sparrow,
heron and herring and hummingbird,
whooping cranes, and bees.
Now our hearts are pounding wildly,
our eyes fill with tears
at the glory of this world—

all in a jumble then, frantically
getting ready for Shabbos, come
antelope and alley cat, Irish setter, polar bear,
black bear, beaver, tiger, squirrel, chipmunk
and camel, lioness and spring lamb, zebra,
elephant, rattlesnake, hippopotamus,
giraffe, monkey, mountain goat—
and just as it's time to reach
into the box at the back of the cupboard
to pull out two candles and find the matches
for *licht bentschen*—

miraculously comes the human
who can strike the match and sanctify
all the work that God has done, eons ago,
and every moment since,

battling *tohu va-vohu*, the chaos
that threatens to once again engulf it all.
Shaken and humbled,
we reach for the match
and the blessing,
full of gratitude
for this holy world.

B'reishit (Hebrew)—the first word of Genesis, rendered in the King James Bible as "In the beginning." Each week a portion of the Torah is read aloud in synagogue, the first reading of the annual cycle beginning with *B'reishit*, the biblical account of the creation of the world.

tohu va-vohu (Hebrew)—primordial chaos, the state of the world before creation.

Shabbos (Yiddish)—the Sabbath, which begins on Friday night at sunset, the time described in Genesis when God completed the creation of the world and rested. In Jewish tradition, humans rest then as well in celebration of creation. The Sabbath is inaugurated traditionally by lighting and blessing two candles.

licht bentschen (Yiddish)—blessing over the Sabbath candles.

Contents

III. *Practice*

IV. *Recognizing a moment of happiness*

Part One

What's known and what needs to be studied

Solstice

Lying in bed,
our limbs intertwined,
anchored and warm under old down,
the night sky still dark
and suddenly, my blood stops.
I can feel the platelets piling up
in the pause, the wave's crest
higher and higher, unnatural—
can blood flow backwards?
And I recognize
my body has turned to fear,
fear in the blood, in the platelets,
waking me, with no memory
of dreaming.

The enemy is time.

What's known and what
needs to be studied

For many years I excelled at sighing,
the sighs I produced were legendary—
people studying in far-off corners
of the same grand old library room
would turn to see the source, the face
of a person who could emit a sound
from such a deep and soulful place.

Once my husband was reading quietly
in our living room and though separated
from me by more than 50 feet and two
closed doors, heard the sigh I sighed
in our bedroom and came in to say,
No one has a right to sigh like that—
he heard my sigh as a demand,

as an aggression, as an intrusion—
it was all of that, but it was more,
it was a plea, a supplication:
is there no one who can help me bear
this heart that will not stop
breaking? For many years I excelled
at sighing, then finally, instead,

learned to breathe. Who would have
imagined that breathing was anything
you needed to learn, to practice,

didn't it just come with the basic equipment,
wasn't it as natural as, well, breathing?
But no, not at all, and I am only just now
beginning to get the knack of it.

A fearsome thing

Most of my life I have given over
to you, and to you, also to you,
always you at the center with me
on the sidelines, the good girl
carefully doing her homework,
doing dishes and worrying, family
errands and worrying, worrying
and thinking, feeling on behalf of
you, then you, finally you.

I was doing what I was supposed
to do, and also—I have to be honest—
it was a fearsome thing,
putting myself at the center.
I had no idea how to do that,
was never instructed—how
to be a woman at her own center.

Only slowly, first in stolen minutes
here and there, in borrowed
or begged-for hours, next in dedicated
days, then in long holiday weekends
I encumbered for myself, finally
in weeks at a time of lustful abandon—

apart from you, you,
even you. In the silence
and spaciousness, tentatively,
someone new emerged,
someone ready finally to dare
fearsome things.

Burning

Now at 57 I could be
such a good mother—
patient, generous, spacious,
parenting with a long view,

absorbing the wild crazed
force field of their tantrums,
offering up an eye of safety
amid infantile chaos, disintegration.

Now at 57 I feel a need
to confess to my dearest
women friends the sins
of long gone days and minutes.

Like Shakespeare's tormented Lady—
though she bears a different guilt,
our hindsight suffering much the same—
no way to right what is wrong.

As if by magic, able at last
to take the long view, I see clearly
through the rear view mirror
the daily anger that burned, burned.

Coming of age

A glorious June day, I'm on the porch reading,
and my son carries a large black Hefty bag
out of the house, out to the garbage,
the muscles of his upper arms straining.

A college graduate for five days now,
living at home with us for one last summer,
he's cleaning his room, discarding emblems
of childhood to make way for the man
he is becoming. But I am the daughter of Depression
parents, and I wonder what is in that Hefty bag,
wonder if a son born of this disposable culture
can make an imaginative leap to Salvation Army
and hand-me-downs, wonder if that Hefty bag
holds anything of value that could be handed down.

I wonder, but understand that pawing through
his garbage is not an option: what is required of me
is patience and respect, a leap of faith,
the capacity to live with uncertainty.

How it crowds out
all the good things of life

for Roger, 1945–1996

I know everything there is to know about pain:
the pain of not being the favorite, the pain
of watching dark moods envelop someone you love,
the pain of longing and longing for what you can't have,
of counting minutes, minute by minute, waiting
for the good thing to happen, waiting for relief.
Pain is slow, it inches along, if it moves at all.

For five weeks I visited my brother in the Norwalk Hospital:
one night, terrible pain, he took himself
to the emergency room. Out of nowhere, a malignancy.
Diagrams on napkins to explain surgical possibilities,
appointing trustees, drawing up a will—just in case.
How can you be 50, with money, a complicated life,
but no will? Only if you knew you'd live forever.

Waiting for the elevator I began to notice a hand-lettered sign,
"Pain Management." Every day, standing in the lobby,
waiting for the elevator, "Pain Management."
And I marveled that in some room or suite
in the Norwalk Hospital was a person or persons
who were expert, who could advise, about "Pain Management."
I promised myself I'd check it out, but it got lost

in the shuffle of investigating drug protocols, hoped-for
surgeries, planning a funeral, sitting *shiva*—beginning to end,
from walking around and playing tennis to dead—5 weeks—

All these years later I never fail to pay my respects—
a special attentive silence, sometimes the sigh,
occasionally quiet tears—even at the wheel
my eyes glaze over passing exit 40 (or is it 39?)
on the Merritt Parkway. It all went so fast,
I never found the support group for spouses,
children, parents, significant others, siblings.

But maybe one day on the Merritt, my curiosity
will rise above cowardice and fear, I'll exit
the highway, let my hands and feet remember
how to find the hospital and see if the sign
is still there by the elevator. I still wonder
what they do, what they teach, in a room or a suite
in the Norwalk Hospital about pain management.

Passover miracle

for Kara

that we find our spring selves again,
shed the thick protective layers of winter
that shield but separate us
from the world out there.

We sit at the seder table
tired, yes, from all the work of preparation,
but hoping to be refreshed,
hoping in spirit to be refreshed.

Sitting at the seder table
we encounter
our younger selves,
wide-eyed, asking questions.

We become each year once again
the four sons, child-like,
spring-like, ready each year once again
to go out from Egypt

with nothing
but a pack on our back,
ready to walk once again
out into the wilderness

in search of our freedom
and our God.

Not yet 75, Ruth

Striding toward the far end of the rocky field,
the olive sapling balanced on her hip—
about the same heft as an eighteen month old—
she surveys the difficult terrain, the raw
November morning, then exercises patience
as she waits her turn for the pick.

She remembers another time, another world,
remembers what it was like to be here then,
working the soil in an infant country,
full of dreams and prayers and innocence.

A full lifetime of striding, balancing life
on her hip, looking for the places to plant life,
life that longs only to be planted and to grow.
Unbelievable, she thinks, that anyone fights
over this soil impervious to shovels, soil
that resists even a pick and a strong stubborn back.

And now, her turn, she digs. Rhythmically
the pick rises and falls, slowly persistence
is rewarded, the hole finally deep and wide enough,
she places the olive sapling in the earth.

But all the hard years have taught her
physical straining is just the beginning
of planting a tree. She stands and waits
for the song and the prayer to rise within her
then tears come too, tears of sorrow
and pain, tears of hope, fierce love.

What more have the hard years taught her?
Be on the lookout for what needs to be done
and for partners—the only hope is shoulder to shoulder;
surrender to the work, persist, especially in rocky soil;

don't give in, don't give up, don't give out
and don't get sentimental—it's a waste of time;
always at the end, listen for the prayer, the prayer that rises
within, listen for the prayer of thanksgiving and the prayer
of supplication—thank you God for the strength to do this work,
thank you God for returning me to this beloved place;

please God, nurture this tender sapling,
grant it long life, let it bear much fruit.
And please God, see our suffering, hear our cries,
help us to find each other—isn't it time yet for peace?

The raw morning is warming. She turns back toward
the truck, striding to bring the next sapling.

In November 2008, an interfaith group of forty Americans traveled to Israel and
the West Bank to support the work of Rabbis for Human Rights. We visited
Israeli and Palestinian human rights and social justice programs and planted trees
at various sites in solidarity with peace initiatives.

Dreaming of home

We want so much to be in that place
where we are respected and cherished,
protected, acknowledged,
nurtured, encouraged, heard.

And seen, seen
in all our loveliness,
in all our fragile strength.

And safe, safe in all our trembling
vulnerability. Where we are known
and safe, safe and known—
is it possible?

Kol Nidre

I am grateful for this,
a moment of truth,
grateful to stand before You
in judgment.

You know me as a liar
and I am flooded with relief
to have my darkest self
exposed at last.

Every day, I break my vows,
to cherish this moment,
to be a responsible
citizen of the world.

No one sees, no one knows,
how often I become distracted,
lose myself, and then lose hope—
every day, every day.

On this day, this one day,
I stand before You naked,
without disguise, without embellishment,
naked, shivering, ridiculous.

I implore You—
let me try again.

Dreaming of breast and milk

for Lisa

He and I were talking about enough,
about how much is enough
and when we know we've had enough—
a subject we've addressed
many times—and suddenly
I remembered looking down at you
when you had finished nursing
and had fallen asleep at my breast.

I remembered the tremble, the after-suck
of moist lips dreaming of breast and milk,
the milky white liquid still pooled in the mouth,
a thin stream dribbling down the chin,
and sometimes the fluttering of closed eyelids,
a blissful perfect sleep, and how still cradling you
in one arm I'd smooth the top of your perspiring
soft head with my other hand.

When in my life before or since
have I felt so perfectly enough.

We no longer need to exchange anniversary gifts

It was all there in your eyes last night,
the clarity that comes from many
long years of looking and loving,
the face so well known it has ceased
to be a face like other faces, like new faces,
by now it is distilled into flesh and skin
pulled across muscle and bone,
and underneath, a beloved animal creature,
more human than human.

Part Two

Leah's house and after

Inside out

for Leah, 1925–1993

Infinite as the stars
are the lines crosshatched
on my arms now.
Stop, I want it
to stop.

Long ago, Leah,
friend of another generation
confided, "They look at me
and see the Dean's wife,
dignified matron, but inside
I'm an uncertain
new mother, inside
there's a young woman's
taste for pleasure, inside
I'm full of wonder
and dancing, inside
I'm shy, not yet 35."

When I look at my arms
now, I think, Leah.

Leah's house

I miss the smell of your house welcoming me
as I came through the door: an aroma distinct
from the wafting of your freshly baked bagels
or the hearty lentil soup you made—not
one of those easily identifiable food smells
gloriously arriving and departing week to week—
no, this was a mysterious scent,
a scent underneath all the others,
like the bass line in a song.

I knew enough in the last years
to cherish it, and truly, I puzzled—
was it the woodwork? the walls themselves?
something you cleaned with?—
and could I, should I, start using it too
so my house could smell like that,
so I could have that special smell of you
to carry with me when some day
you and the house were gone?

I never did ask, and the house is long gone,
as are you, you with your intelligent
questions, your quiet listening
that opened my heart. Sometimes
I tell stories of you, remembering you clearly,
sometimes I understand now who we were.

What remains

for Aaron, 1923–2003

What do we have in the end—
the people we loved,
the people who loved us.

You and I have the times we raked leaves together,
our fingers getting cold and stiff, our cheeks
tough and shiny from the autumn chill.

We have the times I stayed over and slept in the attic,
the old apple tree welcoming me right outside
the third floor window, and the loud crickets at night.

We have the times I made you dinner,
lentil soup and real bread and a candle
on the table in the kitchen,

and the times I used cloth napkins for breakfast,
with homemade bagels from her recipe
to give us a taste of what we had lost.

We have the times I brought my chair right up next to yours,
looked into your blue eyes and demanded,
What's wrong? Where does it hurt?

because I knew it would help you to talk,
and we have the times you answered me honestly,
and the times you squirmed around the truth,

the times you lied outright, the times
I helped you, and the times
you couldn't let me help you.

We have the times we held each other and cried
and were comforted feeling the body of the other close,
breathing in each other's smells.

We have memories of teasing
and stories and running jokes that ran for years,
you insisting I should have ended the play

by killing her, how it wasn't a big Broadway hit
and I didn't get a Tony because I wouldn't
follow your advice and kill her.

I am left with these memories
and memories of countless goodbyes, lingering
together in the doorway, then you standing there

watching as I backed out and drove away,
my heart aching not wanting to go,
and you with tears in your eyes.

I am left with the cradle you made for Uri
and the dollhouse you made for Lisa,
the easel, two bulletin boards, three bookcases,

a small neglected jewelry box
and a cutting board I've used
most every day for 20 years or more.

And now, returned to me by Mike,
I am left with a book of my poems
and other books too, given you for birthdays

and ordinary days, a white sweater extra large
that you always wanted because you never had
a white sweater, so I bought one for you.

But who will I call now on Friday afternoons
to offer a blessing as the sun is setting,
and who will I call now

before the seder to say,
I'll be looking for you
when we all go out from Egypt tonight,

and who will I call now to say,
as the last stubborn snow is finally melting
here in New England,

Coming up this morning in my little front yard garden
there are four daffodils and three red tulips,
and yes, crocuses too.

Holding on

There in the corner of my room
the sweater I gave you
and asked to have returned to me
after you died. What was I thinking?

I didn't plan to wear it,
I only wanted to hold on to you
a little longer, wanted
a possibility for my fingers.

But when I got it back—
something surprising—
it had your smell. And so
for a number of months

I'd scoop it up,
close my eyes, bury
my face in the soft weave,
and breathe.

Almost summer again now,
almost a full year. Today, cleaning,
I pick it up, lower my face
in my hands. Inhaling deeply

I ache that the sweater has finally
let go the smell of you.
What will I do with it now,
now that it's only a sweater?

Heart against the wind

A woman sits in the waiting room in Penn Station,
bouquets of fabric cascading on her lap:
fanciful rose and forest green blossoms in purple fields,
bright yellow squares festooned with cornflowers,
boutonnieres of palest lavender dancing on midnight blue,
a mossy green with shadows of Victorian girls and lads.
She sews, she sews, her hand moves across the quiet rows,
and in her lap the quilt in all its splendor grows.

But on her face a different story: in successive waves
pain opens and breaks and suddenly the needle stills,
large hands at rest, a long deep sigh, eyes no longer
on gaily colored squares but lost mid-air,
welling with tears that do not fall, cannot fall.
If I could be certain of a place beyond this place,
I would leave now and join him there. I hear him calling,
Merle.

While you declined

Why didn't I say healing prayers for you
as I did for others who are still alive now.
Others for whom I prayed on a regular basis
have survived long beyond their diagnoses—
one even has had a revision, a reversal,
of diagnosis. They continued working, went
about their business, vacationed in Europe,
bought new cars, celebrated additional grandchildren,
while you faltered, declined, declined.
Why didn't I pray for you daily, by the hour,
extract from the Universe a softened decree.

The years of your denying you needed anything
from me, your stubborn repeated refusals
to accept the help I offered—they accumulated,
they piled up. And of course we both believed
you were so exceptional, you'd go on forever,
neither of us able to imagine a world without you.
So finally, I succumbed, stopped watching
as if I had the power, through my love, of life
and death, as if I could affect a change, as if
my watching mattered. And then finally, because
what was there in plain sight was too terrible to see.

The visiting porch

for Jean-Claude

My wraparound New England porch is well populated
this early March afternoon, though the temperature hovers
at 40. Sitting with me in the sun is a ten year old girl from Brooklyn
who normally contents herself stretching out on her stoop
with a book and a bunch of grapes, mostly to read
but also to daydream and observe the steady stream of passersby.

With me on the porch as well is the playwright, who as a rule
enjoys his own porch an hour north of here—any day with sun,
any season at all—sits with a laptop, a book, maybe a cup of tea,
reading, writing, daydreaming too. It was from him I learned
to sit on the porch in the sun in any season, even in the cold.
And sometimes I extend our companionable silence

to the gentleman farmer who told me he has occasion once a month
to drive down my street—now and again I peer into passing cars
to see if this is his once a month. What a curious gathering—
me, the Brooklyn girl, two quirky white-haired men, dreamers
and interpreters of dreams—but I'm an excellent host,
well-practiced in making everyone feel right at home.

The walk

We are walking together around the pond,
a mild morning in early spring, and the walk
is muddy in places but that doesn't matter
because the air is kind and alive and we are alive,
enjoying an opportunity for conversation.

How is Hannah? I ask, and she gives me a few
perfunctory words about her daughter,
then politely moves the conversation on to me,
but I know better and ask again. This time
she accepts and opens and tells and soon

her face is distorted, full of color
as she chokes back tears and continues
to talk and walk, then finally, crying,
sobbing, turns and plaintively asks, *How many
times does my heart have to break?*

—you know, like when you're in labor,
you want to know how much more of this
will there be, how do I pace myself—and I
surprise her with an actual estimate, *I'd say
you're six or seven centimeters dilated now.*

And she stops crying and her eyes widen
and she wants to know more—how did I
calculate that—and I respond that slowly, imperceptibly,
the balance shifts and it's time for you to put down
the weight of responsibility so they can pick it up,

and it's not that you stop caring and worrying
and hurting for them, but finally, the burden
of making their choices is not yours anymore,
nor the torment that whatever you chose
was a bad choice, the wrong choice, and the anguish

that you are a bad mother, the wrong mother—
it can subside, it should. Now I stop walking
and she stops walking, I look in her eyes and help her
remember all she's done to nurture this child,
all the hard good work, all the gifts of love,

and I give her a word, *grief,* and she's so grateful—
yes, grief, that's the word—grief that time is passing,
grief that the golden years of baby and little girl
are gone, grief that mistakes have been made,
grief that she is no longer a young mother.

Grief, yes, it's a word with dignity and gravity,
a word that befits this moment, a word that's worthy.
Now as we walk she repeats what I have said
and I repeat what I have said and we are both
grateful for the pond and the walk, for all of it.

In the checkout line

Oh, Joe, if she could see you now,
wouldn't her heart break:
suddenly stooped over and looking lost,
in front of me in the checkout line.
When did you last shave, Joe,
and have you been drinking this morning?

I didn't recognize you, but I knew that voice,
he booms. *Yeah, Brooklyn,* I respond with a laugh,
thinking, I didn't recognize you either,
feeling guilty I've stopped calling to check in.
How's Maggie? I venture. *Ah, bad economy for new grads,*
says Joe, *she's still looking for something full time.*

He asks after Lisa and Uri and then when we're done
with children, his and mine, I name the presence
that has hovered—*I think of her so often, I miss her.*

We all do, says Joe, and after that, can't go on.

I notice, but do not
attempt interpretation

I have a friend whose luck has turned,
after all these years her ship has come in—
a job that pays well, a worthy position
in her field of expertise, contracts for prestigious
and lucrative projects—first one, then two—
necessitating travel to far-off exotic destinations.
And I'm happy for her, and proud—I tell everyone
how well she is doing, and certainly
at the beginning of this new karma
I rejoiced that after all the years of struggle
she finally was enjoying such good fortune.

And yet I notice we speak less often now
and when we do, I notice as she complains
of exhaustion, an unforgiving commute
and the challenge of juggling so many responsibilities,
there's a sadness in my shoulders, a weight
on my chest that results in shallow breathing.
I notice that my listening is less eager
than it was a year ago when her good fortune
was fresh, when ghosts of the many lean hard years
were still lurking in corners, frustrated, angry.

After I hang up I'm in a foul mood, measuring
all the narrow places in my life, thinking *almost*
and *if only*. I remind myself how much I love her,
how talented and worthy and deserving
she is, but still I reach for the phone

less and less now and I avoid wondering
what it means to be the sort of person
who can stick by her friends through miscarriage,
unemployment, divorce, widowhood, chemo, locusts
and death of the firstborn, but uncover so much trouble
bearing witness to an abundant harvest.

The shape of kindness

Because I am a sophisticated traveler
I imagined the shape of your kindness
to be round. Wherever I wandered
across the face of it, I felt secure—
aha, I'd think—a mountain, but still
a kindness, even with its fearful steep incline.
Then, desert intensity, seeking water
and beauty where at first glance the terrain

and sun-white sky are blinding.
Just when my eyes have become
accustomed to the hot light, a roaring
waterfall threatens to sweep me away,
except again, I shore up my courage—
it is just another face of kindness
I say to myself, and push on, curiosity
and confidence feeding one another.

                    Ultimately though
the discovery that wrenches me
from my false security, confirming
what ancient sailors knew: that the earth
is not round, and when you venture beyond
the edges that are known and charted,
you tumble into a depthless abyss
where there is no kindness.

You, standing over me

We ended in the way
that was most comfortable,
most familiar,
for both of us—
me, on the floor,

bloodied, beaten
beyond recognition,
whimpering,
an animal whimpering,
you, standing over me,

the club still in your hand,
blood dripping from the club,
stunned, exhausted
from the fight,
not remembering

how you came to be
holding the club,
not remembering the fight,
just standing there looming
over me, victorious,

guilty, again the perpetrator
of involuntary manslaughter.
You recognize yourself
in this scene,
I recognize myself.

Prolonging silence

The one who prolongs the silence
is the one with power,
and as the silence expands
and extends, the power
expands and extends.

And so I smile
that after all these years
I am suddenly
and unexpectedly
the one with power here.

I am discovering
I like power—
don't guffaw—
I really didn't know
that before.

Choosing silence it turns out
is the opposite of being silenced—
I had vast experience
with the latter, the former
is completely new.

I like it, I like power,
I am just beginning
to explore it, wield it,
just beginning to taste it—
it's delicious!

I'm a long way
from questions of ethics
and responsibility—
I'm still in the power
nursery, practicing

timing, patience, self-discipline.
For now I am concentrating
on not getting dizzy,
not losing my balance,
not spinning out of control.

I withheld nothing

In the end I realize I withheld nothing
from you, not a single ridiculous terror,
not one shy insecurity.

And more: I told the story
of the little wooden child's stool
where I sat listening to the radio,
and how he pulled it out from under me
just before I sat, and how I landed hard
and surprised on the floor and cried,
the first memory of the first cruelty
imprinted hard inside my body.

The story of first lovemaking,
marked also by tears, by an opening,
by a different imprinting. And the story
of how I said goodbye to my mother.
Ugly knotted stories of my secret jealousies,
the little obsessions that sink their teeth in
and mercilessly shake us, impervious
to our whimpering and begging Let me go.

But what's the use in my counting and recounting
how many stories I've recounted, how many
stories I remembered and told.
They were, after all, only stories,
and never held the power to tether you to me.

A door closes

The last time we met
I wish the sun had been shining,
I wish I had been as gentle
with you as with my babies
still wet from the womb.
I wish I had better understood
what you were saying, underneath
the words, and addressed myself
to those underneath words.

I wish you had seen me
once more—a soft woman,
worthy of trust, full
of affection and respect.
Instead you saw—what?—
someone angry, demanding,
dangerous. Instead we sparred,
your heart on guard as if
we had never trusted.

But then the moments
when your eyes were full,
they were saying something—
what? I was so tight, intent
on stories, pulling out of you
stories I thought I needed, deserved,
stories that seemed important.
Instead I should have asked,
What are your eyes saying?

A missed meeting is someone's fault,
isn't it? And the temptation is great
to blame, conclude the fault
was his—if only he hadn't
fought me, if only he had given
what I asked for. And the pain
is great to imagine the mistakes
were mine—if not for me, it all
would have turned out beautifully.

Nearing the end

One question is
should I save you
a place in my heart,
or should I work
to fill the emptiness,
or, alternatively,
allow the wild grasses
to grow over
the bald spot
naturally, as they will,
in their own good time.

Remember me

Inevitably I suppose
you'll remember my hair—
ubiquitous focal point—
though truthfully it doesn't interest me
as much as others might imagine.

I prefer you remember
the timbre of my voice,
how it comes filtered
through the sounds of stoopball
and Brooklyn corner candy stores;

how fiercely I listen,
my head cocked to one side,
how readily I open
the storehouse
of my undistracted attention;

how I relish
teasing out a laugh,
extending the line on it,
reeling it in, then playing it out again
before finally cutting it loose.

But remember especially, please,
the moments when everything
particular about us fell away,
when you and I breathed together
with one beating heart,

like sisters under the same roof
sharing a single cycle of blood.

Part Three

Practice

Early telling

I woke up early
with the birds—
in fact, they woke me—
their chatter, and the light.

As my father used to ask
when I'd come home from school,
walk in the door
and reach for the phone
to call the friend
I had just spent the day with,

incredulous, he'd demand,
*What can you have
so much to talk about?*

So too now, I wonder—
what is that flurry
of early morning
bird conversation?

Young ones,
telling dreams.

The winter body

How I wait for the ritual
of bringing the bucket of sand
that has sat all winter by the porch steps
back into the house, down
to the cellar till next year.

How I wait for the hallelujah
when dead earth cover begins to go green,
when the New England April air
finally softens, yielding
to a faint spring mist of a rain.

And now I become aware of the tension
I've been holding behind my eyes, in my hands,
at the top of my broad shoulders,
in my belly and the calves of my legs,
the hard grinding working of my jaw.

What is my body's equivalent
of the bucket of winter sand
brought back down to the cellar?
So hard, to let go, longing
to be the spring porch.

Practice

for Rosalie

Open your hand, the small muscles
that have a surprising will to tighten,
to contract, to make a claw, a fist—
determine to release all those small
tight hard muscles—relax them,
relieve them, be attentive and tender
toward them. And as you open them
they will help you to open
the large long muscles of the forearms,
those long muscles that work so hard
to protect your chest, those long muscles
of the forearms that guard and isolate
your heart. Slowly, with great care,
move your head back and forth,
back and forth, easing, opening
the tightness in the neck, and yes,
open your mouth wide, open and close
your mouth and release all the tension
you hold in your jaw, back and forth
roll the head and release the tired mouth,
the tired neck, the tired jaw.

Quite naturally then the shoulders
can square, drop and square, drop and square
and the shoulder blades will be so grateful
to melt down into your back. And now the heart
can find an opening, the heart wants
to open and rest and breathe.

You are surprised at the tears pooling
in the corners of your eyes, you think,
I didn't know there were tears waiting there,
but don't stop to think about the tears,
don't analyze them or try to name them,
just allow yourself to enjoy
the breathing, the open beating heart,
the long muscles and the small muscles
of the hands, the forearms, the shoulder blades,
the neck, the mouth, the fierce and vulnerable
open beating heart.

Watching for signifiers

We all know Pavlov's dogs came
to salivate when the bell was rung,
knowing the food would be there,
anticipating the food.

But did they also come to anticipate
the bell itself, did they wait,
did they listen, for the sound of the bell
before the sound came?

Funny, after all this time, I can't
remember if you say, *Our time
is up now*, or, *We have to stop now*,
can't remember the words,

but I do watch to see, I do
anticipate, when you begin
to move your body forward
to the edge of the chair, the sign

that the words are coming.

Unfulfilled promise

I guess I thought you'd lead me
to the promised land, but finally
I realize I never had a vision

of what that would look like,
or what it would feel like
to be free and whole at last.

All I had was confidence in you
as scout, trailblazer, trustworthy
and steady guide. I had faith

you'd take me the whole way
and deliver me safely
to the other side.

And now, we stand together
at the crossroads,
and you tell me,

I've come as far as I can with you,
I've taught you whatever I know
about how to find water

in a wasteland, how to build
a temporary shelter, how to read
the sky, the stars, the trail and the winds.

I look to the horizon
but all I see ahead of me
is more wasteland.

Alone

Sometimes it's delicious
being alone, the bed already neatly
made on my way to the bathroom
to brush my teeth,
the pan and plate washed
right after the breakfast omelet.

On those mornings I examine
the calendar on the fridge
with an irritated squint, begrudging
any interruption, distraction,
social obligation.

On those mornings I want
my solitude to stretch out
over the horizon of the day,
leaving me free and light for interior
adventures that startle, delight,
move me to tears of new awareness.

Then all at once the elasticity
of time spent alone stretches me
back to powerless
moments of childhood,
moments in which I had
and have still no words.

In another solitary agony,
I find myself at the mercy
of a succession of partings
and abandonments,

a parade
of people I have loved
walking down a long corridor
for the final boarding call, each
turning briefly to wave at me
one last time before
disappearing from sight.

In a small spiral notebook

Some days the best you can do
is to be a moving target—make a long list
in a small spiral notebook of all the projects
you need to move along—you know—
send the play to that off-beat theatre in NY,
check out prices of Mexican tile at Home Depot,
print out the book proposal Sandy emailed,
call to wish Jan a happy birthday,
call to see if Larry is OK after surgery,
call to see how Annie is doing with radiation,
email Marc to ask if he wants me to teach
this year. It's genuinely a long list
and on a hard day you can find a lot more
to add to it and then when it's a page or two long
you just start working your way down the list.
It helps to schedule a small reward—
at noon I'll go to yoga and in the late afternoon
I'll plant the flat of purple pansies in red clay pots
or I'll watch a rerun of *Judging Amy*. Or both.
Anything to numb you from the ever hovering
knowledge that you have to say goodbye,
and say goodbye, and then finally, say goodbye.

G
i
d
d
y

We're
paying three men
to wash the windows
of this hundred year old house.
They arrive just before 9, greeted
at the door by Eddie.   Then, upstairs
in my study with   the door closed—
I began my work day half an hour ago— I hear
all over the house windows being pushed up and down,
quickly, proficiently, as screens are removed,   small
air conditioners removed,   and the men prepare to do
the work itself.   Now we are more or less   hermetically
sealed.   I try to ask a question   or two—   I see on this floor
some windows   where screens remain— but   the men
want   no conversation with me and curtly   respond,
We do this all the time lady.   *OK,* I smile, and
back off, feeling a   giddy excitement that this   morning,
Eddie,   the hundred year old house and I will be moving
through a car wash together,   windows rolled up tight,
antennae pushed all the way   down. And then they
did it the old-fashioned   way, by hand, with rags.

Out of time

A Chinese man, maybe 45,
walked past my porch this morning,
talking. I looked for the cell phone
but his hands, his ears,
were free.

Then, ten feet behind,
a woman, matronly
in a cotton dress, dark hair
cut straight at the neck, a pleasant
face with glasses, responding.

And so they proceeded,
out of earshot, out of sight.

Nosegay

When I woke this morning
I was eidelveiss,
I was baby's breath,
buttercups and violets.

I was surprised
and pleased
to face the day
as such a nosegay.

Later the sun
will threaten,
I will look expectantly
for midday shade.

But now, early morning,
I exult in the dew
as it glistens
on my petals.

Child of God

for Jan Uhrbach

Finding her place at the center
of the prayer room, she sends her roots deep,
tapping pure wellsprings at the core of the earth.
Squares her shoulders, opens
chest, face, throat, lips, heart,

releasing ancient words
that have lived inside her forever.

Slowly, quickly, quicker still, fervent, rhythmic,
slow once more, the words and their melodies
fill the room. The large white tallis itself
is in motion as her fist keeps time, and opens,
the open hand, giving, receiving,

searching, exploring, imploring,
interrogating, celebrating, spirit open, alive.

Great bird, magnificent wing span—she soars, swoops,
soars, dives, soars, soars. All this we learn from her:
rooting, tapping, opening, releasing,
giving, receiving, exploring, imploring,
interrogating, searching, celebrating, soaring, soaring.

Child of God, she finds
her place, and we, with her.

People ask

How are you,
what are you doing?

I say, *I'm wrestling*
with my demons.
Sometimes I wrestle them
to the mat, sometimes
they wrestle me to the mat.

In the end, if it gets published,
then we call that writing.

I'm told Adam Phillips understands

Now even the pen feels
too technologically advanced,
only a pencil will be capable
of finding the narrow door
behind which monsters
and demons cavort—yes,
call them wild things.

Only the pencil has power
now to vanquish their
jagged teeth dripping
with your young blood,
the claws that first
ripped your child flesh
and then reopened, reopened

those wounds, never giving
them a chance to heal
properly.   The pencil,
that forgiving tool of childhood,
equipped at one end
for telling and naming,
equipped at the other
to redress all the mistakes
you were expected to make.

Intimate friend, modest
and democratic—everyone
after all can afford
a pencil.   Naming and telling,

telling and naming, and then
erasing, emending, emending,
erasing, the words rocked
in a hammock strung
from heart to mind, words

rocked, rocked, then ready—
sprung, released on the page,
telling secrets, surprising,
nursing the courage to open
narrow doors, the courage
to crane the neck all the way back
and look wild things
squarely in the eye.

There's only one question

And the only answer
is to keep crying,
to cry daily,
the way one
is supposed to
write daily,
or pray daily,
as a discipline.

Part Four

Recognizing a moment
of happiness

She visits

for Lillian, 1910–1976

With tears, a woman of 70 says to me,
I miss my mother (gone now two years)
and I think—bitterly?—what should I say
whose mother died 30 years before,
when I was not yet 30?
*Do I miss you, do I remember you
well enough to miss you?*

The next morning I wake with a vision
so clear—in the last hour of sleeping
and dreaming, you were with me, vivid,
real. Ferociously, I exclaim in my sleep,
This is not a dream! then, urgently,
Where have you been?

You, quietly, not missing a beat, *I've been away.*

The details

for Roger

Isn't it strange, I can't remember if he was
already completely covered with the sheet
when I walked in the room—if I had to remove
the sheet from his face—or if his face was uncovered
and I covered it in the end, or if it was uncovered
and I left it uncovered and they covered it
when they came in to take him away.

It seems like it shouldn't matter,
such a small detail really. I only
bring it up because I'm surprised
and unhappy to realize though it's only
been five years after all,
I don't remember every single detail.

A few months before, reading new poetry of mine
in part about the childhood we shared, he marveled,
How do you remember all these details from so long ago—
or do you make them up, invent them?
Remembering's not hard, I said, it's part of the process:
I reenter a moment to write about it, and in that quiet place
of memory, the details return to me.

It was Saturday afternoon and I remember
getting the phone call—*Should we resuscitate? It doesn't say*
on the chart—agitated, a resident on weekend duty—
We've worked on him 10 minutes—should we keep trying?—

agitated, uncertain, wanting to escape his burden.
I hesitate, then remember how hard Roger has fought—
Yes, yes, keep trying, I'm on my way.

In the parking garage the attendant was miffed
not to have had his hour's notice. I insist on driving myself—
I need to be doing something, and besides, I'm the faster driver,
and besides, I know the route by heart. The whole way up,
over and over in my mind, *Don't let him be a vegetable, please God,
don't let him be a vegetable,* and *There's no reason to have
the funeral in Brooklyn,* and *I'm sitting shiva at home this time.*

Getting off the elevator, I am afraid, suddenly aware
how precious our ritual has become, these daily visits,
his cheery hello, his brightening when I enter the room—*Hi there!*
Now begins the part where there's so much
I can't remember: Did they see me before, and tell me
he was already dead? Did I walk in the room
and find it empty, and have to look

for him in another room? Was he lying there
in his own bed, still and already stiff,
and I realized on my own? The only thing I clearly
remember is when I was ready to say goodbye,
and kissed him on the forehead, the feel of his flesh
on my lips was already stiff and cold—
less than an hour, already stiff and cold.

But I'm not certain about that even: Was it a kiss
on the forehead, or did I touch his hand?
Was it his hand that felt stiff and cold
on my fingers, or his forehead on my lips?
No one else in the room, just Roger and me,
so it's my memory or nothing.

The carousel

for Milton, 1910–1989

And the angel of the Lord appeared unto him
in a flame of fire out of the midst of a bush,
and he looked, and behold, the bush burned
with fire, and the bush was not consumed.
                                        Exodus 3:2

I feel such sorrow to realize only now
the significance of my father waving
as I came around on the carousel,

time and again, each time I made my circuit
on the carousel—ten times? fifteen? twenty?
Sunday morning after Sunday morning,

each time, the smile and wave
that answered
my smile and wave.

Didn't it mean *I love you,*
didn't it mean *we are connected,*
I know this girl, she is mine.

Yes, the large girl with the thick auburn braids,
I acknowledge her, she is mine—
in public, I acknowledge her.

How did I not see,
the wind on my face,
the sentimental tinny music in my ear—

how did I not see
it signifies
he loves me?

In that apartment

In that apartment
there wasn't enough
space or privacy,
hope or heat.

Too few mirrors, not enough
good luck or tenderness,
no perceptible change,
daring, confidence.

There was too much
chocolate, togetherness, fear,
too many roaches, relentless
worrying, silence.

We had music
from the radio,
Camelot, The King and I.
We had my mother's smile.

Under the circumstances
we did the best we could.

Evenings at home

There's nothing like the silence
of family silence: people
connected by blood or love,
habit or longing, occupying
a confined space together
in the same endlessly prolonged
moments in time, each
with their own thoughts,
their own breathing, each wondering
what is in the mind of the others,
each wondering who knows what,
wondering what words are safe words,
searching for a word that might
be a healing word, methodically,
systematically rejecting word after word
as knowing too much, as dangerous.

Night after night the silence grows,
the silence grows as the families
on TV go BLAH BLAH BLAH BLAH
and the real words of consolation,
fury, affection, resentment,
questions of clarification
and points of order fall
to the floor and accumulate there—
a thickening deepening carpet
of unspoken words, until finally
the late night news and people rise,

making their way through the carpet
of unspoken words, murmur
to one another *Good night,*
take themselves to solitary beds
and mute haunted dreaming.

A 9-ounce Nestle bar

passed between us in the evenings.
Sometimes with almonds, sometimes
without. Thick little blocks
of chocolate that melted slowly
on the tongue. Patience was learned
as you waited while the small
square dissolved in your mouth,
slowly quite slowly with only
the mouth's passive moisture
and an occasional subtle movement
of the tongue to tease the process
to its conclusion.
Much the same patience as is
practiced waiting for that adult
explosion of pleasure—the trusting
relaxed attentive waiting
for an explosion of pleasure.

I learned most of what I know
about pleasure sitting
in my living room at the age of 8
in the company of my parents
and older brothers with a small
square of Nestle chocolate
dissolving in my mouth.

Special days

As best I can recall
our custom was to wait
until the honoree
finished up in the bathroom.

Then when you emerged
into the small foyer
that served as dining room
for the miniature apartment,

the family would sing
in unison. There were presents
and cards on the table and we all
sat together as birthday girl

or boy, anniversary couple,
followed the prescribed routine:
first cards that had come
in the mail, then family card

and gift, family card and gift.
Though the demands
of the new day pressed, extra
minutes opened to allow the ritual

its dignity. Wrapping paper
recycled many times,
presents modest,
most often utilitarian—

the real gift was to find
yourself for a few morning
minutes the center
of friendly family attention.

Aunt Julie in our doorway

Making fun of Aunt Julie was a family sport,
her wide open face beckoning like a target,
the large twin circles of her spectacles
forming a double bullseye, offering no protection
to the pale watery eyes behind them, eyes
that seemed perpetually surprised by the casual cruelties
of her siblings and their spouses, perpetually
surprised that even their well–brought up children
finally couldn't bring themselves to laugh
along with her as she laughed and laughed.

Hers was a distinctive laugh, like a small summer
waterfall, little peals and gales, falling and falling
and then starting at the top all over again.
A gay laugh, a child's laugh, a laugh from high
in the throat, she laughed as if she had no
alternative, as if laughter and confusion were all
that God had given her to choose from.

And then at the end of every visit, Aunt Julie
in our doorway. It's common to describe someone
as "lingering in the doorway," but that's not it at all—
Aunt Julie took up residence in the doorway,
planted herself there and effectively resisted
any effort to uproot her. This too, of course,
became a set piece when riffing on the peculiarities
of Aunt Julie—Aunt Julie and her long goodbyes.

How far a journey was it after all—
three city blocks to her own small apartment,
back to the coarse widower who had taken her
for wife, taken her to wash his underwear, mind
his daughter, scrub the linoleum, have supper
on the table. Fifty years later I wake up remembering
and finally understand: *There's something
I came for and didn't get, something I need.*
So hard to leave without it.

December 25

When I was a child in Brooklyn I wasn't jealous
of all the presents they got (though there was a special
doll I always yearned for). I wasn't jealous of the cheerful
fir tree in their living rooms (though the thought of that
incredible smell permeating your city apartment was enticing).
I wasn't jealous of their holiday songs taking over the airwaves—

I loved those songs, I sang those songs, they were my songs,
too, weren't they? (I also was an American, yes?)
And surely I wasn't jealous of their ridiculous Santa Claus—
I can say *that* with complete certainty (though I did envy
the way *their* holiday was *the* holiday, how it took over
everything, the countdown to *their* holiday).

But the real ache, the real regret, the thing they had
that I wanted, was the story. The story where a baby
was important, where a baby was everything.
A baby from a poor family and everyone came to adore him.
The baby was at the center, and the baby would grow up
to be everything, to change everything.

I envied them that their god was a god you could see:
everywhere there were pictures of Him—in museums,
in churches, in magazines, on bedroom walls.
There he was—a baby! There he was—in a manger!
There he was in his mother's arms, there,
at the center, being adored, walking on water,

distributing bread, at the head of the seder table,
dying, suffering, out in the open, his suffering
was out in the open. Dying in his mother's arms.
He cared enough to pay a visit, he cared enough
to suffer and die for them. Unbelievable—you could put him
in your mouth, feel him on your tongue, you could swallow him.

For all these things, a child in Brooklyn, I envied them.

Leaving Egypt

The night is so dark
and I am afraid.
I see nothing, smell nothing,
the only reality—
I am holding my mother's hand.

And as we walk
I hear the sounds
of a multitude in motion—
in front, behind,
all around,
a multitude in motion.

I have no thought of tomorrow,
now, in the darkness,
there is only motion
and my mother's hand.

Catching up to you

for Lillian

Now you and I can be sisters at last—
wasn't that what we always were,
really, though then it was improbable—
a woman with white hair, lined face,
a girl on the cusp of adolescence, teetering.

But weren't we sisters when we pulled
the heavy shopping cart together, weren't we
sisters when we did the dishes at night, singing?
And oh, when we danced the polka
around the miniature apartment, surely
sisters then too. And when you told me
your heartaches, the small details
of where you hurt and how.

Now, finally, I have lived a large life,
all but the third act. I have myself entered
your last decade, joined you now finally,
at the end, sisters in our sixties.

Still dreaming of home

And isn't that what nesting
is all about, that creative urge
when a new baby is on the way,
the urge men mock
or marvel at—

the drive to make a place
protected and pleasing—
we need that bit of fresh paint
and calico. As the body prepares
for the big day of crowning

and pushing, the heart and the hands
prepare a home, full of hope
that this time around
the human family
will not fail.

Recognizing a moment
of happiness

Along Brooklyn streets my mother and I
pulling the heavy shopping cart,
singing together from *Oklahoma*...
Splashing in the sunlight of the community pool,
Lisa's arms then Uri's clasped fast
round my neck as the water cools us,
as we dunk and giggle, dunk and giggle...
With Leah at that Shaker table in her kitchen,
she puts aside the knitting
to listen more intently.

I passed through such moments of happiness
unscathed, all the while doggedly clutching
in my tight fists anticipated catastrophes
and the crumbs of tragedies
I could neither have averted nor remedied,
unable or unwilling to just
let the fear and pain fall
from my fierce grip, unable or unwilling
to loosen my tight grip lest a single crumb
of pain escape. Only now

does it seem I am finally willing
and sometimes able to relax my hands,
unclench the tight fists, to open,
and finally embrace

the happiness shining through
special moments and moments ordinary.
Only now do I finally understand
that all along the choice was mine,
even on terrible days—remain a prisoner of terror,
or dare to celebrate the sunlight on the grass.

Acknowledgments

So much love and generosity have made it possible for me to bring
this volume of poetry to completion: Deep thanks always to my first
and last readers, Eddie Feld and Gail Reimer. Gratitude to Leighton
McCutchen for compassionate listening and masterful interpretation
of dreams; to Ilana Kurshan for enlightening and delightful trans-
Atlantic workshopping of some poems; to Hara Person for early
encouragement; and to Michael Goldberg for kindness, professional
acumen, and patience. Above all, I will forever cherish the many days
on the porch with poet Sharon Dunn, without whom these poems
could never have reached their truest expression—Sharon, my friend,
you have been my teacher.

"B'reishit" was written in honor of Ari Kagan, in celebration of his
becoming a bar mitzvah on Shabbat B'reishit 2007; the poem appears
in *Mahzor Lev Shalem* (Rabbinical Assembly Press, Rabbi Edward Feld
editor) 2010, ©Merle Feld 2007.

An earlier version of "Passover Miracle" appears in *The Women's Seder
Sourcebook* (Jewish Lights) 2003, ©Merle Feld 2010.

"Not yet 75, Ruth" was written in celebration of the 75th birthday of
activist/philanthropist Ruth Schulman, ©Merle Feld 2009.

An earlier version of "Kol Nidre" appears in *Mahzor Lev Shalem*
(Rabbinical Assembly Press, Rabbi Edward Feld editor) 2010, ©Merle
Feld 2010.

"What remains" was written in memory of Aaron Lemonick and was
read in the Princeton University Chapel during his memorial service

About the Author

MERLE FELD'S poetry can be found in numerous anthologies and prayer books and in her highly acclaimed memoir, *A Spiritual Life: Exploring the Heart and Jewish Tradition* (State University of New York Press, revised edition 2007). Her award-winning plays include *Across the Jordan*, published by Syracuse University Press in the anthology *Making a Scene*, and the now classic *The Gates are Closing*, performed in hundreds of synagogues worldwide as preparation for and enhancement of the High Holiday experience.

Feld has facilitated Israeli-Palestinian dialogue on the West Bank and at Seeds of Peace, and has traveled to work with Jewish women activists in the former Soviet Union through Project Kesher. She serves as Founding Director of the Albin Rabbinic Writing Institute, established in 2005, guiding rabbis-in-training across the denominations to develop and explore their own spiritual lives and to serve more effectively as spiritual leaders. A popular scholar-in-residence nationally, Merle and husband Rabbi Edward Feld, who often collaborate professionally as teachers, mentors and consultants, make their home in Western Massachusetts.